Herberts Dorbe

Calm Beasts

illustrated by
Gita Treice

Translated by Žanete Vēvere Pasqualini
and Kate Wakeling

modern nursery rhyme from Latvia #002

two tigers,

five lions more.

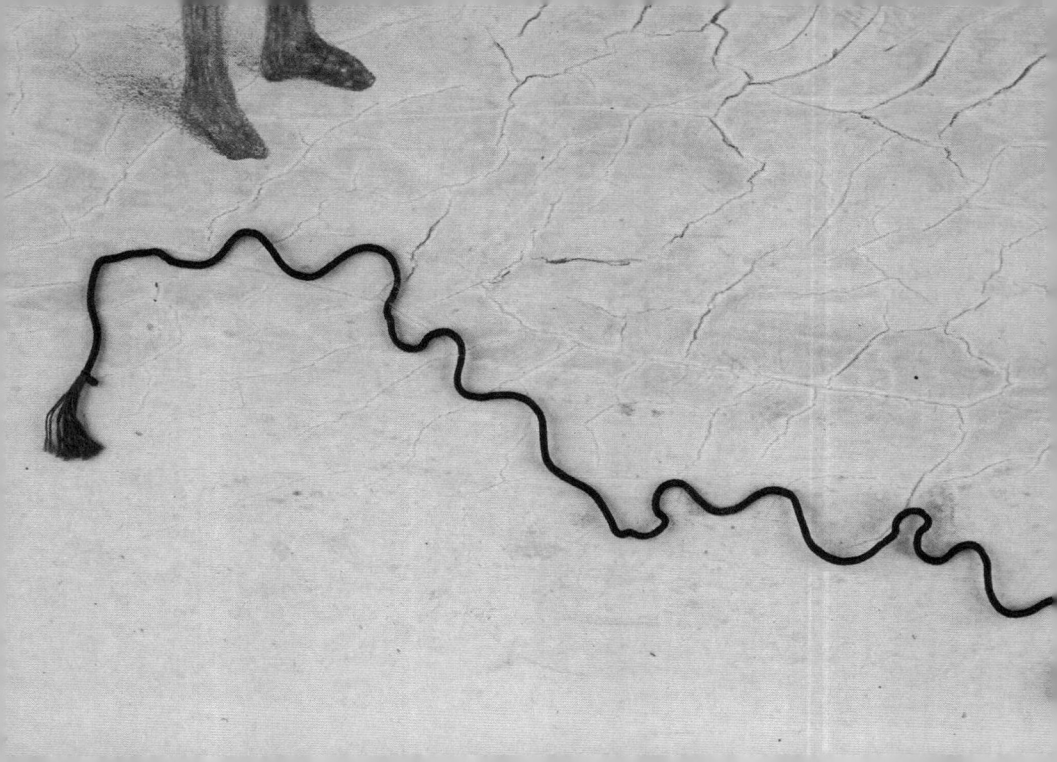

No bars, no ropes,
no lock on the door.

I tickled their backs,
 I tickled their ears,

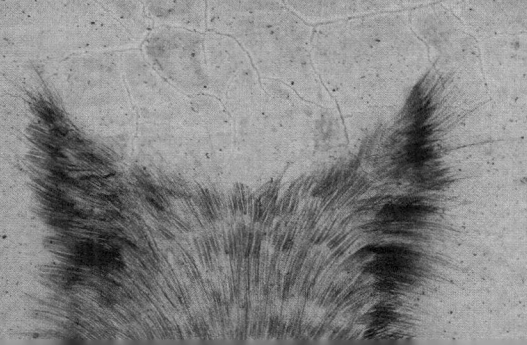

I found myself curiously free of all fears.

They were calm as could be,

no roaring, no howling.

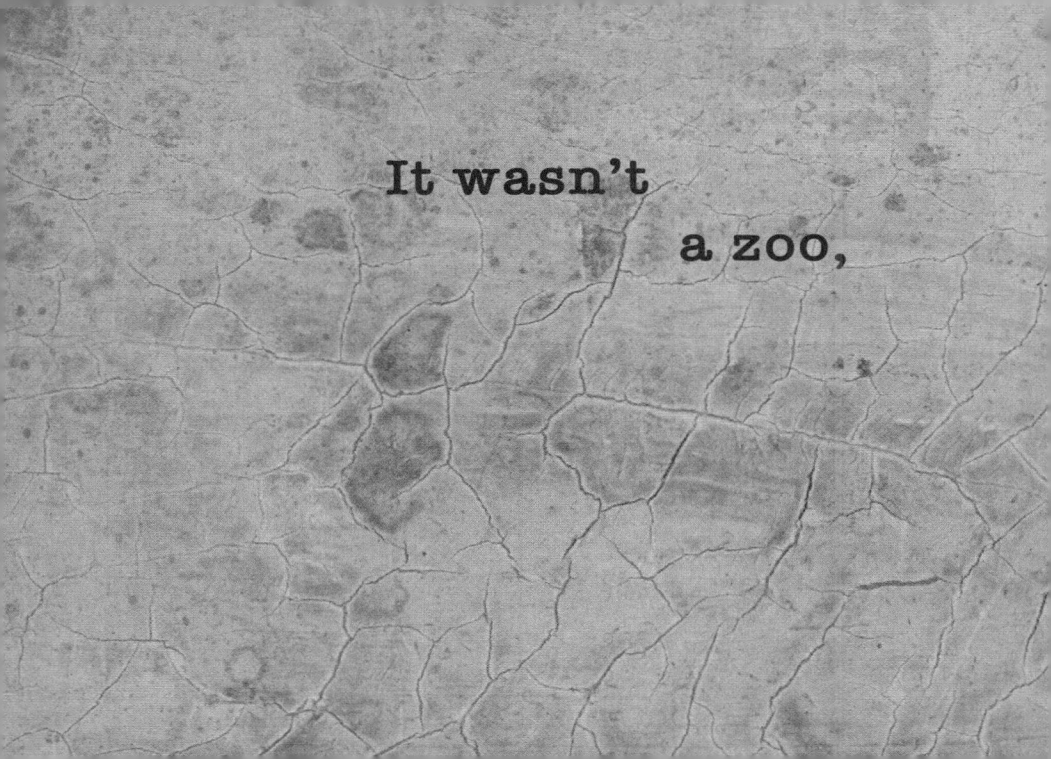
It wasn't a zoo,

nor a dream I mistook.

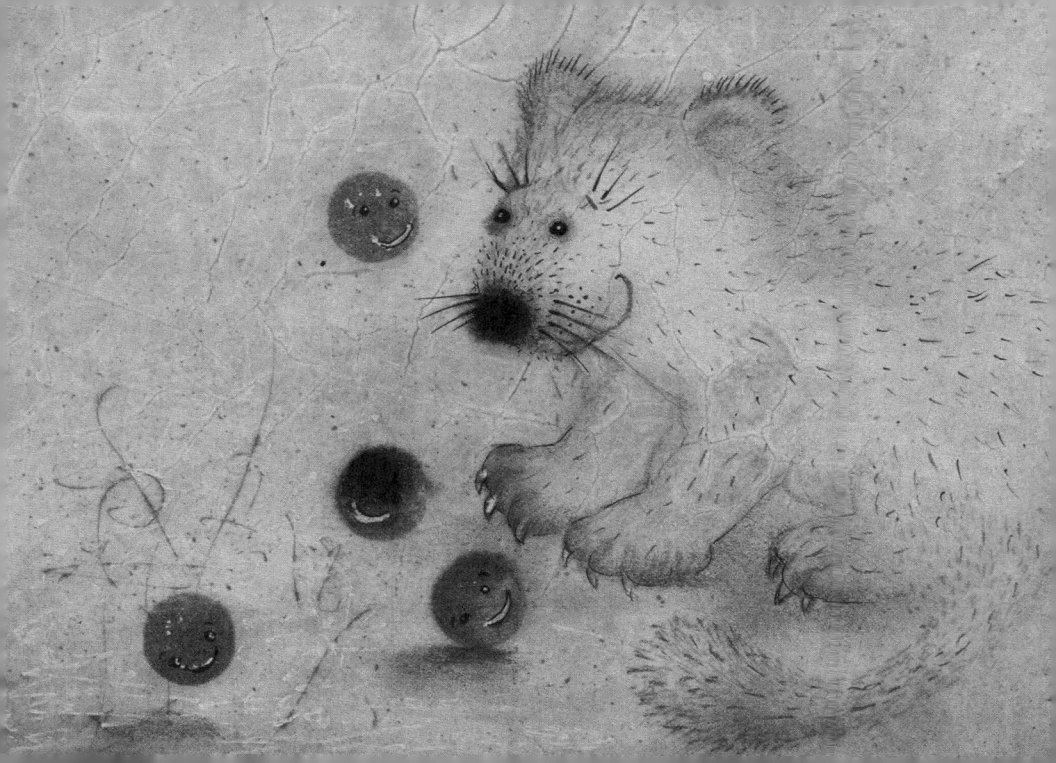

In a picture book.

Supported by Latvian Writers' Union (*Latvijas Rakstnieku Savienība*)
and Ministry of Culture of the Republic of Latvia

Kultūras ministrija

First published in the UK in 2018 by the Emma Press, Birmingham
Originally published in 2013 as "Rāmi zvēri" by Liels un mazs, Riga, Latvia

Text © Herberts Dorbe, 1930
English-language translation © Žanete Vēvere Pasqualini and Kate Wakeling, 2018
Illustrations © Gita Treice, 2013

BICKI-BOOKS
Artistic director – Rūta Briede
Design – Rūta Briede and Artis Briedis

Printed in Latvia by *Talsu tipogrāfijā*
on *Munken Lynx Rough* 150 gsm and *Munken Lynx Rough* 300 gsm

A CIP catalogue record of this book is available from the British Library
All rights reserved.

ISBN 978-1-910139-93-6
theemmapress.com